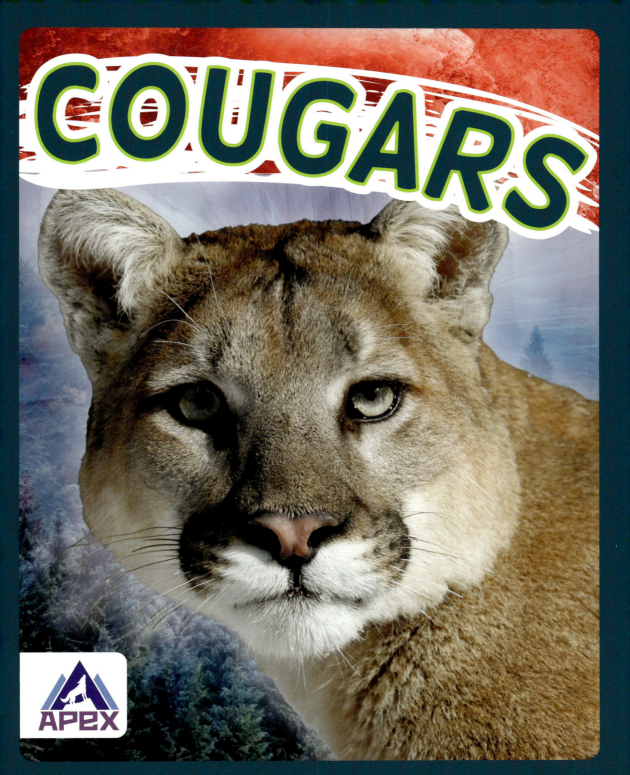

COUGARS

BY Sophie Geister-Jones

WWW.APEXEDITIONS.COM

Copyright © 2022 by Apex Editions, Mendota Heights, MN 55120. All rights reserved. No part of this book may be reproduced or utilized in any form or by any means without written permission from the publisher.

Apex is distributed by North Star Editions:
sales@northstareditions.com | 888-417-0195

Produced for Apex by Red Line Editorial.

Photographs ©: Shutterstock Images, cover, 1, 10–11, 13, 20–21; iStockphoto, 4–5, 6–7, 8–9, 12, 14–15, 16–17, 18–19, 21, 22–23, 24–25, 26–27, 29

Library of Congress Control Number: 2020952947

ISBN
978-1-63738-029-1 (hardcover)
978-1-63738-065-9 (paperback)
978-1-63738-133-5 (ebook pdf)
978-1-63738-101-4 (hosted ebook)

Printed in the United States of America
Mankato, MN
082021

NOTE TO PARENTS AND EDUCATORS

Apex books are designed to build literacy skills in striving readers. Exciting, high-interest content attracts and holds readers' attention. The text is carefully leveled to allow students to achieve success quickly. Additional features, such as bolded glossary words for difficult terms, help build comprehension.

TABLE OF CONTENTS

CHAPTER 1
A GREAT LEAP 5

CHAPTER 2
LIFE IN THE WILD 11

CHAPTER 3
STRONG BODIES 17

CHAPTER 4
HOW COUGARS HUNT 23

Comprehension Questions • 28
Glossary • 30
To Learn More • 31
About the Author • 31
Index • 32

CHAPTER 1

A GREAT LEAP

A cougar races along a cliff. His paws dig into the ground. He hurtles forward. His long tail sticks out behind him.

Cougars can sprint up to 50 miles per hour (80 km/h).

Suddenly, he reaches the cliff's edge. A wide, empty space lies ahead of him. The cougar leaps across it.

A cougar's strong legs help it jump long distances.

A cougar can jump straight up into the air. It can leap 18 feet (5.5 m) off the ground.

Cougars are good at climbing trees.

He flies through the air. He stretches out his long body. Then he lands safely on the other side.

MANY NAMES

Cougars once lived all over North and South America. People in different places made their own names for the cat. These names include puma, panther, mountain lion, and catamount.

CHAPTER 2
LIFE IN THE WILD

Cougars have a huge **range**. They're found in the western parts of North America. They live in South America, too.

Cougars can live as far north as British Columbia, Canada.

Many cougars live in forests or mountains. But they can survive in many different **habitats**. Some live in **swamps** or deserts.

Cougars in colder areas often have thicker fur.

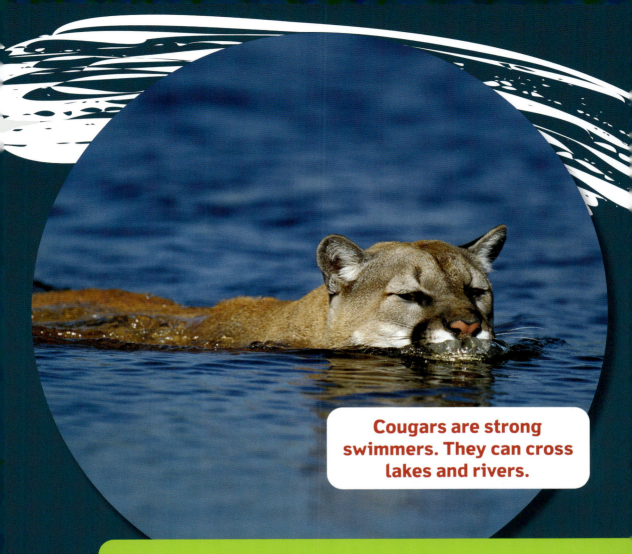

Cougars are strong swimmers. They can cross lakes and rivers.

CITY CATS

Like most wild animals, cougars avoid humans. However, more people are moving into areas where cougars live. As a result, people may sometimes spot cougars in cities.

Cougars are solitary animals. Most live alone. Cougar cubs stay with their mother for about one to two years. Then they go live on their own.

Cougars mark their territory with poop or urine. The smell tells other cougars to stay away.

Mother cougars teach their cubs how to hunt and find food.

CHAPTER 3
STRONG BODIES

A cougar's fur is tan. Its belly is white. It has black markings on the tip of its tail, ears, and nose. These markings help the cougar blend in with its **environment**.

Cougars have round faces and big, gold eyes.

Cougars can climb trees to avoid danger.

Cougars are big cats. They weigh 80 to 180 pounds (36–82 kg). They have strong legs and long tails.

Cougars cannot roar. Instead, they purr, hiss, growl, and scream.

Cougars use their long tails to balance while they run or jump. They swing their tails from side to side.

A cougar's body is often 3 to 5 feet (1–1.5 m) long.

A cougar's back legs are longer than its front legs. This helps the cat jump.

Cubs have spots for about six months.

STAYING SAFE

When cougars are cubs, their fur has dark spots. The spots are **camouflage**. They help the cubs hide from **predators** while their mother hunts.

CHAPTER 4
HOW COUGARS HUNT

Cougars are excellent hunters. They can catch moose, deer, and other large animals. But they also eat smaller **mammals**, such as raccoons.

Cougars walk very quietly while they hunt.

A cougar can kill its prey with a single bite.

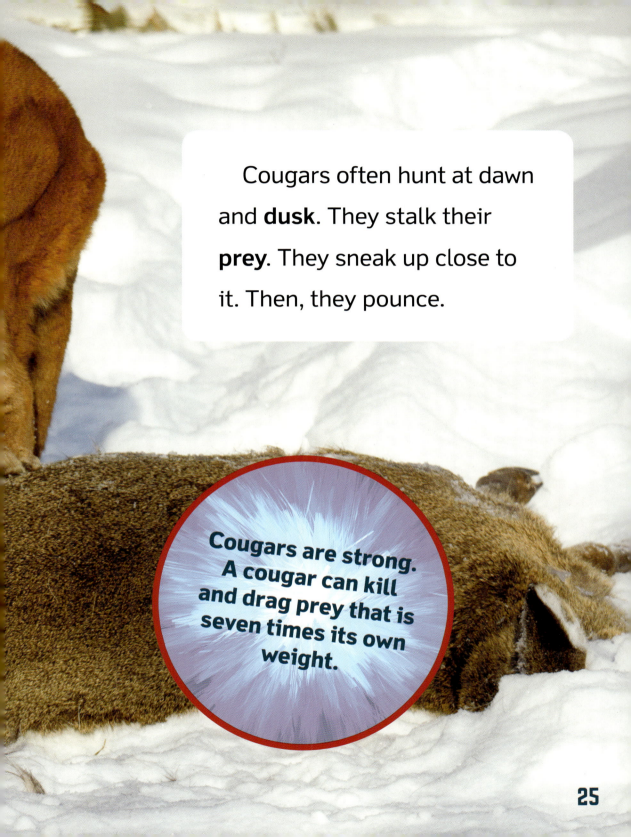

Cougars often hunt at dawn and **dusk**. They stalk their **prey**. They sneak up close to it. Then, they pounce.

Cougars are strong. A cougar can kill and drag prey that is seven times its own weight.

Cougar teeth are built to cut and tear.

A cougar bites its prey's neck to kill it. The cougar's sharp teeth tear easily through meat.

FEEDING TIME

Cougars do not eat every day. When cougars kill large prey, they hide it. They feed on it for several days. They eat the entire animal. Afterward, cougars may go days without eating.

COMPREHENSION QUESTIONS

Write your answers on a separate piece of paper.

1. Write a sentence describing how cougars hunt their prey.

2. Would you want to live near a cougar? Why or why not?

3. Why do cougars swing their tails?

    A. to balance while they run
    B. to mark their territory
    C. to catch their prey

4. How does camouflage help cougar cubs stay safe?

    A. It makes the cubs harder for predators to find and eat.
    B. It helps the cubs find more food without their mother.
    C. It helps the cubs run faster.

5. What does **solitary** mean in this book?

*Cougars are **solitary** animals. Most live alone.*

    A. living in large groups
    B. staying away from others
    C. being very dangerous

6. What does **stalk** mean in this book?

*They **stalk** their prey. They sneak up close to it. Then, they pounce.*

    A. to move slowly and loudly
    B. to move quickly away from something
    C. to move quietly toward something to surprise it

Answer key on page 32.

GLOSSARY

camouflage
Colors or markings that help animals blend in with the area around them.

dusk
The time of day just before night when the sky gets dark.

environment
The surroundings of living things in a particular place.

habitats
The places where animals normally live.

mammals
Animals that have hair and produce milk for their young.

predators
Animals that hunt and eat other animals.

prey
An animal that is hunted and eaten by another animal.

range
The part of the world where an animal can be found.

swamps
Areas of low land covered in water, often with many plants.

territory
An area that an animal or group of animals lives in and defends.

TO LEARN MORE

BOOKS

Abdo, Kenny. *Black Panthers*. Minneapolis: Abdo Publishing, 2020.

Hogan, Christa C. *Mountain Lions*. Lake Elmo, MN: Focus Readers, 2017.

Sommer, Nathan. *Lion vs. Hyena Clan*. Minneapolis: Bellwether Media, 2020.

ONLINE RESOURCES

Visit **www.apexeditions.com** to find links and resources related to this title.

ABOUT THE AUTHOR

Sophie Geister-Jones lives in Saint Paul, Minnesota. She loves reading. She and her brothers have a book club.

INDEX

C
cities, 13
cubs, 14, 21

E
ears, 17

F
forests, 12
fur, 17, 21

H
habitats, 12
hunting, 21, 23, 25

J
jumping, 7, 20

L
legs, 19–20

M
markings, 17
mountain lion, 9
mountains, 12

N
North America, 9, 11

P
prey, 25, 27
puma, 9

S
South America, 9, 11
spots, 21

T
tail, 5, 17, 19–20
teeth, 27
territory, 15

Answer Key:
1. Answers will vary; **2.** Answers will vary; **3.** A; **4.** A; **5.** B; **6.** C